GRAPHIC LIBRARY™

THE APOLLO 13 MISSION

by Donald B. Lemke

illustrated by Keith Tucker

Consultant:
James Gerard
Aerospace Education Specialist
Kennedy Space Center

Capstone
press

Mankato, Minnesota

Graphic Library is published by Capstone Press,
151 Good Counsel Drive, P.O. Box 669, Mankato, Minnesota 56002.
www.capstonepub.com

092011
006366R

Library of Congress Cataloging-in-Publication Data
Lemke, Donald B.
    The Apollo 13 mission / by Donald B. Lemke ; illustrated by Keith Tucker.
    p. cm.—(Graphic library. Disasters in history)
    Includes bibliographical references and index.
    ISBN-13: 978-0-7368-5476-4 (hardcover)
    ISBN-10: 0-7368-5476-2 (hardcover)
    ISBN-13: 978-0-7368-6871-6 (softcover pbk.)
    ISBN-10: 0-7368-6871-2 (softcover pbk.)
    1. Apollo 13 (Spacecraft)—Accidents—Juvenile literature. 2. Space vehicle accidents—United
States—Juvenile literature. I. Tucker, Keith. II. Title. III. Series.
TL789.8.U6L33 2006
629.45'4—dc22   2005028477

Summary: In graphic novel format, tells the dramatic story of the rescue of the Apollo 13
    astronauts.

Art Direction
Jason Knudson

Graphic Designers
Juliette Peters and Jason Knudson

Production Designer
Alison Thiele

Colorist
Kim Brown

Editor
Tom Adamson

Editor's note: Direct quotations from primary sources are indicated by a yellow background.

Direct quotations appear on the following pages:
Pages 5, 7, 9, 10, 11, 13, 23, 24, 25, 26, from Apollo 13 PAO Mission Commentary Transcript
    (http://www.jsc.nasa.gov/history/mission_trans/apollo13.htm).
Pages 14 (top panel), 15, 22, quoted in Failure Is Not an Option by Gene Kranz (New York:
    Simon & Schuster, 2000).
Pages 14 (bottom panel), 17, 19, 20, quoted in Lost Moon by Jim Lovell (Boston: Houghton
    Mifflin, 1994).

TABLE OF CONTENTS

Chapter 1

Houston, We've Had a Problem

In 1961, President John F. Kennedy challenged NASA to land a human on the moon. Many Americans believed the goal was impossible. But on July 20, 1969, the crew of *Apollo 11* touched down on the moon. Four months later, *Apollo 12* did it again.

As the decade ended, NASA hoped its exploration of the moon was just beginning.

Good luck, gentlemen.

Bring us back some moon rocks!

On April 11, 1970, Commander Jim Lovell led his crew into the *Odyssey* command module of *Apollo 13*.

10...9...8...7...

Ready, Freddo?

After four years of training, I'm as ready as I'll ever be.

Odyssey connected to the service module. The service module contained fuel, oxygen, and a rocket to get back from the moon.

6...5...4...

The command and service modules rested high atop a Saturn V rocket. Lovell rode the rocket on one of his earlier three space missions.

3...2...1...0

For Fred Haise and Jack Swigert, this flight would be their first trip into space.

We have liftoff.

At 1:13 in the afternoon, *Apollo 13* lifted off from Kennedy Space Center in Florida.

Saturn V was built in three parts called stages. As the rocket shot into space, each stage fell off when it ran out of fuel.

KKKKRRRRR!

Houston, this is Apollo. We've separated from the second stage and we're firing the third.

Teams of flight controllers monitored the spacecraft from Mission Control in Houston, Texas. During the launch, Joe Kerwin was in charge of the Capcom team. Capcom radioed messages between the controllers and the crew.

Roger, Apollo. Everything looks good.

Let's head for the hills!

At 3:38, the crew ignited Saturn V's final stage, blasting *Apollo 13* toward a hilly part of the moon called Fra Mauro.

Less than two hours later, the astronauts separated the command and service modules from the Saturn V.

BANG!

The *Aquarius* lunar module (LM) was tucked inside the rocket. The crew needed this small spacecraft to land on the moon.

Okay, I'm firing thrusters to turn Odyssey around.

As command module pilot, rookie astronaut Swigert was in charge of connecting *Odyssey* to *Aquarius*.

We are just about there—

Got it, Houston!

—about 10 more feet now.

With *Aquarius* attached, *Apollo 13* continued its journey to the moon.

7

11

Chapter 2

Solving the Problem

We're shaking around up here, Houston. I'm having trouble controlling this thing.

Fuel cells one and three are dead.

Houston, oxygen tank number two is reading zero.

Those numbers can't be right.

Oxygen tank number one level is falling.

All of those systems couldn't break down at the same time!

In Houston, Kranz knew what the astronauts suspected. Without oxygen, the crew wouldn't be able to breathe, and the spacecraft couldn't create power.

Now let's everybody keep cool. The LM is still attached.

They can use it as a lifeboat until we figure out a way to get them home.

Let's solve the problem, team.

With 15 minutes of power left, Mission Control ordered the crew to shut down the *Odyssey* command module and move into the *Aquarius* lunar module.

Let's hope this thing turns back on when we need to get home.

I didn't think I'd be back here this soon.

Just be happy it's here to come back to.

The astronauts could use *Aquarius* as a sort of lifeboat. Its small supply of power and oxygen would keep them alive.

14

Five and a half hours after the explosion, Mission Control had a plan. On April 14 at 2:43 in the morning, the astronauts fired the *Aquarius* engine.

I really thought when we started up this engine we'd be landing on the moon.

So did I.

The 30-second burn put *Apollo 13* on a path around the moon and back toward earth.

Carbon dioxide from the astronauts' breath had built up inside *Aquarius*. Soon, the spacecraft would be filled with the poisonous gas.

There aren't extra carbon dioxide filters for Aquarius. We didn't plan on the three of you being in there this long.

We've got some guys working on the problem, Jim.

Well, we can't hold our breath for the next two days.

With little time to spare, a team at Mission Control invented a way to use the *Odyssey* filters in *Aquarius*.

The carbon dioxide levels are dropping!

Well, it's not pretty, but it works.

With carbon dioxide levels back to normal, the crew could do little more than try to stay warm. The temperature inside the spacecraft fell to 38 degrees.

The cold can't be good for the equipment.

We'll find out now. It's time to power up the command module for reentry.

21

On the morning of April 17, the astronauts moved back into *Odyssey*, the only part of the craft designed for reentry. Moisture from the astronauts' breath clung to the spacecraft's cold walls and windows.

These instrument panels are pretty wet. What's the chances of them shorting out?

It doesn't matter at this point. We really have no other choice.

At 7:14, the crew released the damaged service module into space. As it floated away, the crew caught their first glimpse of the damage.

There is one whole side of the spacecraft missing. The whole panel is blown off, almost from the base of the engine.

The crew had little time to think about the damaged service module. Three and a half hours later, they released one more part of the spacecraft.

LM jettison.

We owe our lives to that ship.

Farewell Aquarius, and we thank you.

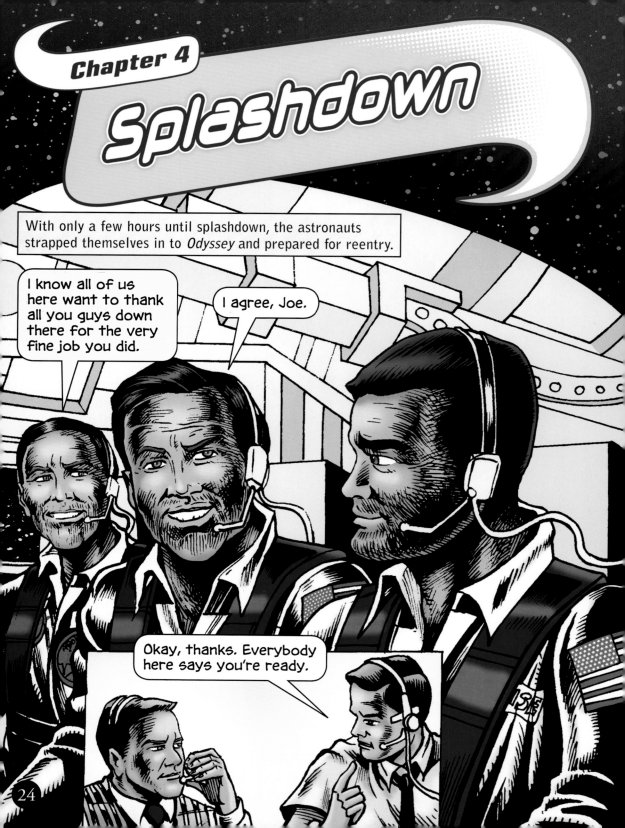

Chapter 4
Splashdown

With only a few hours until splashdown, the astronauts strapped themselves in to *Odyssey* and prepared for reentry.

I know all of us here want to thank all you guys down there for the very fine job you did.

I agree, Joe.

Okay, thanks. Everybody here says you're ready.

24

For the next three minutes, the astronauts would be unable to communicate with Houston. The heat from reentering the atmosphere blocked out all radio signals.

If Odyssey's heat shield has been damaged, the spacecraft will never survive reentry.

After four and a half minutes, Mission Control and the rest of the country still waited. No one knew if the astronauts had made it.

Odyssey, Houston standing by, over . . .

Odyssey, Houston standing by, over . . .

The *Apollo 13* mission was called a successful failure. The crew failed to land on the moon. But they successfully guided a damaged spacecraft back to earth.

In the months to come, NASA fixed the problems discovered on *Apollo 13* and completed four more missions to the moon.

More About Apollo 13

 Three days before the mission, Jack Swigert replaced astronaut Ken Mattingly as *Apollo 13* command module pilot. Mattingly had been exposed to an illness called the German measles. Doctors worried he would become sick while in space. Mattingly never got sick and helped flight controllers during the rescue mission.

 The Saturn V rocket launched all of the Apollo moon missions. It was the largest rocket ever used by NASA, standing 60 feet taller than the Statue of Liberty.

 Only five minutes after launch, the *Apollo 13* mission nearly ended. The first stage of the Saturn V had fallen off, and the second-stage engines were burning smoothly. Then suddenly, one of the engines shut down. Flight controllers at Mission Control acted quickly. They burned the remaining engines a little longer and saved the mission.

 The command module's display panel included 24 instruments, 40 indicators, 71 lights, and 566 switches.

During the rescue, Lovell, Haise, and Swigert limited their drinking water. By the end of the mission, each member of the crew was severely dehydrated. Commander Jim Lovell lost nearly 14 pounds. The crew lost a total of 31.5 pounds during their nearly 6 days in space.

 On April 14, the U.S. Senate adopted a resolution asking for all businesses and media to join in prayer for the safety of the astronauts.

 After a long investigation, the *Apollo 13* Accident Review Board identified the cause of the explosion. Damaged wires shorted out and caught fire inside oxygen tank 2. Within seconds, the tank exploded. The explosion damaged oxygen tank 1 and part of the service module.

 The *Odyssey* command module of *Apollo 13* is on display at the Kansas Cosmosphere and Space Center in Hutchinson, Kansas. Visitors to the museum can view the vehicle that kept the astronauts alive during reentry.

GLOSSARY

broadcast (BRAWD-kast)—a TV or radio program

Capcom (KAP-kom)—the flight control team on the ground that radios messages to the astronauts

carbon dioxide (KAR-buhn dye-OK-side)—a gas with no color or odor; people breathe this gas out.

jettison (JET-uh-suhn)—to throw out something that is no longer needed

module (MOJ-ool)—a separate section that can be linked to other parts

ration (RASH-uhn)—to give out in limited amounts

reentry (ree-EN-tree)—the return of a spacecraft through earth's atmosphere

splashdown (SPLASH-doun)—the landing of a spacecraft in the ocean

INTERNET SITES

FactHound offers a safe, fun way to find Internet sites related to this book. All of the sites on FactHound have been researched by our staff.

Here's how:

1. *Visit www.facthound.com*
2. Type in this special code **0736854762** for age-appropriate sites. Or enter a search word related to this book for a more general search.
3. Click on the **Fetch It** button.

FactHound will fetch the best sites for you!

READ MORE

Beyer, Mark. *Crisis in Space: Apollo 13.* Survivor. New York: Children's Press, 2002.

Graham, Ian. *You Wouldn't Want to Be on Apollo 13!: A Mission You'd Rather Not Go On.* New York: Franklin Watts, 2003.

Marcovitz, Hal. *Reaching for the Moon: The Apollo Astronauts.* Explorers of New Worlds. Philadelphia: Chelsea House, 2001.

Pierce, Alan. *Apollo 13.* American Moments. Edina, Minn.: Abdo, 2005.

BIBLIOGRAPHY

Apollo 13 PAO Mission Commentary Transcript. National Aeronautics and Space Administration. Johnson Space Center. http://www.jsc.nasa.gov/history/mission_trans/apollo13.htm

Cooper, Henry S. F. *Thirteen, the Apollo Flight that Failed.* Baltimore: Johns Hopkins University Press, 1995.

Godwin, Robert, ed. *Apollo 13: The NASA Mission Reports.* Burlington, Ont.: Apogee Books, 2000.

Kranz, Gene. *Failure Is Not an Option: Mission Control from Mercury to Apollo 13 and Beyond.* New York: Simon & Schuster, 2000.

Lovell, Jim, and Jeffrey Kluger. *Lost Moon: The Perilous Voyage of Apollo 13.* Boston: Houghton Mifflin, 1994.

INDEX